LIFE IN STRANGE PLACES

Dark Secrets
life without sunlight

Harry Breidahl

This edition first published in 2002 in the United States of America by Chelsea House Publishers, a subsidiary of Haights Cross Communications.

Chelsea House Publishers
1974 Sproul Road, Suite 400
Broomall, PA 19008-0914

The Chelsea House world wide web address is www.chelseahouse.com

Library of Congress Cataloging-in-Publication Data Applied for.
ISBN 0-7910-6614-2

First published in 2001 by
Macmillan Education Australia Pty Ltd
627 Chapel Street, South Yarra, Australia, 3141

Copyright © Harry Breidahl 2001

Edited by Angelique Campbell-Muir
Text design by Cristina Neri
Cover design by Cristina Neri
Desktop publishing by Katharine Shade and Cristina Neri
Illustrations by Rhyll Plant
Printed in China

Acknowledgements
The author and the publishers are grateful to the following for permission to reproduce copyright material:

Cover photographs: Radiant light background, courtesy PhotoDisc; sulphur-feeding bacteria, courtesy Photolibrary.com/Prof. Jim Watson/SPL; crabs at deep sea vent, courtesy Auscape/© Ken Smith Laboratory, Scripps Inst. Of Oceanography — Oxford Scientific Films.

Auscape/Jaime Plaza van Roon, p. 6; Auscape/© Ken Smith Laboratory, Scripps Inst. Of Oceanography — Oxford Scientific Films, pp. 1, 15 (bottom right); Auscape/NASA/Tsado — Tom Stack, pp. 7 (top), 23 (top), 28 (middle); Australian Picture Library/Corbis, pp. 5 (top left), 5 (bottom right), 12, 13 (both), 19 (top), 20, 21 (top), 24, 29 (middle); Dr. Cindy Lee Van Dover, p. 27 (top); Eurelios/© B. Malaize/ExtrA PoL, pp. 5 (bottom left), 22, 29 (right); Harry Breidahl, p. 7 (bottom); Henry Aldrich, University of Florida, pp. 5 (top right), 21 (bottom right); National Oceanic and Atmospheric Administration/Department of Commerce/OAR/National Undersea Research Program (NURP), pp. 3, 4 (both), 10, 11 (top), 15 (top left), 16, 17 (both), 25, 26, 29 (left); Photolibrary.com/Hulton Getty, p. 28 (left); Photolibrary.com/Prof. Jim Watson/SPL, pp. 11 (bottom), 14; The Picture Source/J.A. Pisarowicz, pp. 18–19; The Picture Source/M. Rohde, p. 23 (bottom); © Woods Hole Oceanographic Institution, p. 27 (bottom); Woods Hole Oceanographic Institution/© Tom Kleindinst, p. 28 (right).

While every care has been taken to trace and acknowledge copyright the publishers tender their apologies for any accidental infringement where copyright has proved untraceable. Where the attempt has been unsuccessful, the publishers welcome information that would redress the situation.

Contents

SEARCHING THE WORLD WIDE WEB FOR LIFE WITHOUT SUNLIGHT

If you have access to the world wide web, you have a gateway to some fascinating information. You can also use the web to see photographs, watch short videos and even search for particular topics. In this book, useful search words appear like this— hydrothermal vents. Useful books and web sites are also listed on page 30.

Introducing life without sunlight

Although we generally take the Sun for granted, it is vital to almost all life on Earth. This is because the Sun provides energy for nearly all living things. On land, plants trap sunlight and use it to make their own food. Animals also rely on the Sun, whether they eat plants or other animals that eat plants.

It was once believed that the Sun was the only source of energy for all life on Earth. However, it has recently been discovered that some living communities can survive without the Sun. Such communities have been found in the deep sea, in caves and in rocks deep below the Earth's surface.

HOW DO YOU SAY IT?

hydrothermal: **hi**-drow-**thur**-mal

In 1977, tube worms and clams were found clustered around deep-sea **hydrothermal vents**. This showed that living communities could survive without the Sun's energy (see pages 12–15).

Other deep-sea communities were discovered by *Johnson-Sea-Link* (shown here) in the Gulf of Mexico in 1984. The creatures in these communities relied on natural gas rather than the Sun for energy (see pages 16–17).

In 1986, a cave was discovered in Romania that was totally sealed from the Sun and the rest of the world. Surprisingly, this cave was full of weird animals (see pages 18–19).

Only a few years ago, no one believed there could be any sort of life deep below the Earth's surface. However, there are subterranean microbes (microbes that live below the surface of the Earth) that can survive in this **environment** (see pages 20–21).

Scientists in Antarctica have discovered a lake below almost 4 kilometers (2.5 miles) of ice. They think there may be life here (see pages 22–23).

Because life without sunlight is hard to find, scientists who study this life need special equipment, such as deep-sea submersibles (see pages 24–25).

Background
Using the Sun to make food

All **organisms** need two things to survive. They need energy and materials to build and maintain their bodies. Food provides both of these things. Although all life on Earth needs food, only some organisms are capable of making their own food. These organisms are called autotrophs. Plants, including trees, grasses, ferns and mosses, are autotrophs that rely on the Sun to make food.

The green color of plants is produced by a chemical called chlorophyll. Chlorophyll is usually found in a plant's leaves where it is used to turn sunlight into food. This process is known as **photosynthesis.** Without the Sun and photosynthesis, plants would not be able to survive. But the story does not end here— the Sun and photosynthesis are important to almost all life on Earth.

HOW DO YOU SAY IT?

autotroph: **ort**-o-trof
chlorophyll: **klor**-a-fil
photosynthesis: **fo**-toe-**sin**-th-e-sis

On land, plants are the main organisms that carry out photosynthesis. Photosynthesis is a chemical process that relies on sunlight to combine carbon dioxide (a gas) and water, to make sugars (food) and oxygen.

This is a photograph of the Sun's surface. The energy released by the Sun provides food for almost all life on Earth.

Plants are not the only autotrophs that carry out photosynthesis. In the sea, algae, such as the seaweeds shown here, can use the Sun to make food. Some **bacteria** are also autotrophs.

Passing food along the chain

Not all life on Earth is able to make its own food. Organisms that rely on other living things for food are called heterotrophs. Animals are heterotrophs. Almost all animals on Earth feed, either directly or indirectly, on plants or other organisms that carry out photosynthesis. In this way, the food made during photosynthesis keeps almost all animals alive.

A food chain shows us how food is passed from one organism to another. Almost all food chains start when plants, or other photosynthetic autotrophs, convert sunlight into food. Animals that eat plants (herbivores) are the next link in the chain. Further links in the chain occur when animals eat other animals (carnivores).

A MARINE FOOD CHAIN

Sun

phytoplankton
(plant-like plankton)

krill

whale

A TERRESTRIAL (LAND) FOOD CHAIN

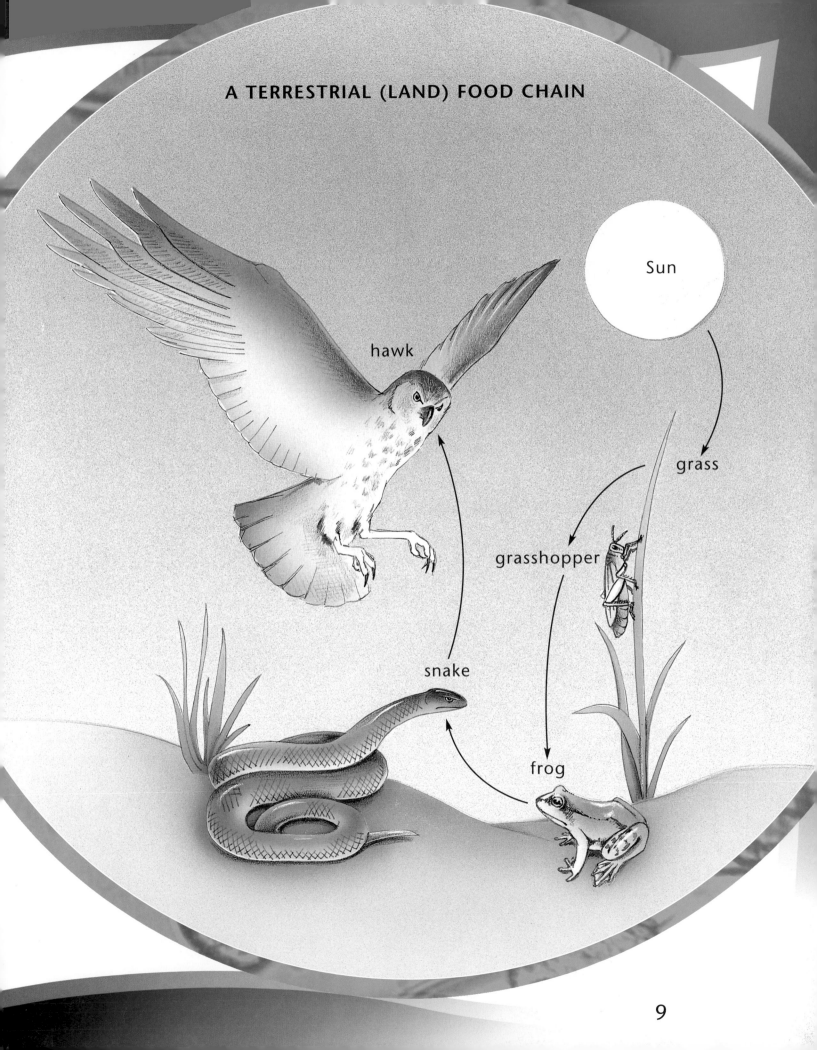

Making food without the Sun

Some autotrophs use another process, called chemosynthesis, to make food. Chemosynthesis relies on chemical energy rather than sunlight. The only organisms that can carry out chemosynthesis are **microscopic**. These incredibly small organisms are commonly called microbes. Many chemosynthetic microbes are bacteria that belong to a group called the **Archaea**.

Just 30 years ago, scientists had not yet begun to explore Earth's totally dark places. The deep oceans had hardly been visited by humans, and scientists had not thought to look for life in rocks deep within the Earth. Nevertheless, life can exist in these dark places. Chemosynthesis and the bacteria that carry it out are the keys to this life without sunlight.

HOW DO YOU SAY IT?

Archaea: ar-**kee**-ah

chemosynthesis: **kee**-moe-**sin**-th-e-sis

Chemicals, such as the foul-smelling **hydrogen sulphide**, provide the energy for some autotrophs. Hydrogen sulphide is found in volcanoes and ⚙ hydrothermal vents in the deep sea.

It was only recently discovered that animals can eat chemosynthetic bacteria. In dark places, such as the deep sea, food chains start with these bacteria. These are food chains that do not rely on the Sun.

In chemosynthesis, bacteria (like the one shown here) use carbon dioxide and water to produce sugars (food), but they do not produce oxygen. Bacteria use these sugars to provide energy and materials, which they need to build and maintain their bodies.

11

Vent microbes

The deep-sea vent discovered by *Angus* and *Alvin* in 1977 was called Clambake 1 (because there were clams around the vent and the water was very hot). When scientists opened the first Clambake 1 samples, they found the water smelled like rotten eggs. This smell was caused by hydrogen sulphide, a gas that comes from inside the Earth. The gas is forced out of the Earth's crust with the hot water that streams out of the hydrothermal vents at 350^0 Celsius (650^0 Fahrenheit).

Hydrogen sulphide can be poisonous to the organisms that live on the Earth's surface, but it is vital to the organisms that live around hydrothermal vents. Hydrogen sulphide is the energy source for the whole community. Microbes, mainly bacteria, are the autotrophs of this community. These autotrophs use chemosynthesis to make their own food. They are the beginning of a food chain that depends on hydrogen sulphide (chemical energy) rather than the Sun (light energy).

Microbes are the first step in a deep-sea-vent food chain. Most of these vent microbes belong to a group of bacteria called the ✴ Archaea. These microbes are also called extremophiles because they live in an **extreme environment**.

Giant tube worms clustered around deep-sea hydrothermal vents eat vent microbes. Large clams and mussels also eat vent microbes. They are the second step in a deep-sea-vent food chain.

Crabs, shrimp, fish and octopuses eat the tube worms, clams and mussels that live around hydrothermal vents. They are the third step in a deep-sea-vent food chain. This deep-sea food chain was the first food chain discovered that is totally independent of the Sun.

Gas-powered mussels

A different kind of deep-sea community was discovered by accident in 1984. Biologists were using nets to study an area where oil and natural gas **seep** through the sea floor. They were working in water over 600 meters (2,000 feet) deep, so they did not expect to find much life. When they brought their nets back up to the surface, they were surprised to find them full of mussels and tube worms. Using the submersible ✈ *Johnson-Sea-Link* to get a closer look, they found mussels living around pools of very salty water. They also found masses of long tube worms living nearby.

Very salty water is known as brine. The mussels that *Johnson-Sea-Link* found were crowded around a pool of brine that sits on the sea floor. A gas called **methane** seeps up through the sea floor and into the brine. This methane is the energy source for the whole community. Like the deep-sea-vent communities, microbes that use chemosynthesis start the food chain in these brine-pool communities. Here, however, the chemosynthesis is powered by methane rather than hydrogen sulphide.

The submersible *Johnson-Sea-Link* on the surface of a deep-sea brine pool surrounded by mussels. Methane that seeps up through the brine is the energy source for this community.

Chemosynthetic microbes live inside these brine-pool mussels. These microbes use methane to make food, which is also used by the mussels. In turn, other animals around the brine pool feed on the mussels.

Johnson-Sea-Link also found that the oil and gas that seeps from the rocks is changed into hydrogen sulphide by the microbes. The microbes that live inside tube worms use this hydrogen sulphide to make food.

17

Life below the Earth's surface

Blind spiders and transparent scorpions

Another discovery of life without light was made in 1986 in a cave near the Black Sea, in Romania. The cave is 25 meters (80 feet) underground. It had been cut off from the rest of the world for five million years. When cave explorers first lowered themselves into the cave they found that it smelled of rotten eggs. More surprisingly, the cave was crawling with all kinds of weird creatures, such as blind spiders and transparent scorpions. This was the first community found on land that does not get its energy from the Sun.

The rotten egg smell came from hydrogen sulphide inside the cave. Microbes that use this hydrogen sulphide as an energy source form a scum on the surface of water at the bottom of the cave. The animals living in the cave feed, either directly or indirectly, on these microbes. Over 50 different kinds of cave animals live in this way. They survived because there was an energy source (hydrogen sulphide) within the cave and autotrophs (microbes) that use this chemical energy to make food.

Although this cave in Mexico is not completely sealed from the outside, it also has food chains that rely on hydrogen sulphide. The structures on the cave's roof have been named snottites. They are made by microbes, which use hydrogen sulphide to make food.

18

Although dark, most caves are linked to the outside world. But the Romanian cave discovered in 1986 is isolated from all other life on Earth. The animals found in the Romanian cave live completely without light or food from outside. Instead, they feed on microbes that rely on rotten-smelling hydrogen sulphide for energy.

Lithotrophs

Microbiologists only recently began studying rocks brought to the surface by drills. They also began to explore deep mines. These scientists were surprised to find microbes living inside rocks deep below the Earth's surface. In fact, they have found so much life in subterranean rocks that they now think there may be as much life underground as there is on the surface of the Earth.

Some subterranean microbes feed on **organic** material that either seeps down from the surface or may have been trapped in rocks when they formed. So these microbes rely on food that was originally made at the Earth's surface. Another group of microbes is made up of autotrophs that make their own food using **hydrogen** found in the rocks. These microbes are called ✪ lithotrophs, a word that means 'rock-eater'. Very little is known about lithotrophs. They survive in very extreme conditions, and they are very different from the more familiar microbes found on the Earth's surface.

HOW DO YOU SAY IT?

lithotrophs: **lith**-o-trofs

Microbiologists can explore subterranean environments in deep underground mines. Some mines, such as this gold mine in South Africa, are as much as 3 kilometers (1.8 miles) deep. Sunlight never reaches this far underground, so chemosynthesis is the only energy source for the microbes that live here.

Scientists use drills that can reach thousands of miles into the Earth's surface. The drills bring rock samples back up to the surface for scientists to study. Scientists search for subterranean microbes inside these rocks.

Microbes from deep within the Earth are incredibly small. New types of rock-dwelling microbes are being discovered all the time. They survive in extreme environments, with high temperatures, and without sunlight and oxygen.

Icy microbes

One of the most remarkable searches for microbes living without sunlight is happening in the coldest place on Earth—Vostok Station in Antarctica. Almost 4 kilometers (2.4 miles) below the ice at the Russian Vostok Station lies ✈ Lake Vostok. It is 224 kilometers (140 miles) long and up to 484 meters (1,600 feet) deep. This hidden lake was first detected and mapped by radar, and is thought to be between 500,000 and one million years old.

To find out if there is life in Lake Vostok, microbiologists began drilling down through the ice. They found microbes living in the ice 3.5 kilometers (2 miles) below the surface of Vostok Station. How these microbes survive in such a cold and dark environment is still a mystery. However, the microbiologists had to stop drilling just 120 meters (400 feet) above the lake, because they did not want to contaminate the lake with microbes from the surface. Nevertheless, the fact that the microbes were found so close to Lake Vostok means it is possible there is life in the lake itself.

Lake Vostok is almost 4 kilometers (2.4 miles) below Vostok Station, in Antarctica. It is not yet known if life can survive in this cold and dark environment.

The icy crust of Jupiter's moon ✈ Europa appears similar to Antarctica, and it is possible that there may be an ocean beneath Europa's ice. Therefore, **astrobiologists** looking for life beyond Earth are interested in whether or not there is life in Lake Vostok.

These incredibly small bacteria (1 micrometer, or one-millionth of a meter) were found in ice 3,590 meters (11,850 feet) below Vostok Station. Are there similar microbes living in the lake?

Technology
Submersibles exploring inner space

It is fascinating to think that humans landed on the Moon before they discovered life around deep-sea vents. This happened because the exploration of Earth's extreme environments, such as the deep sea, is not an easy task. The vehicles used to explore the deep sea are like spacecraft, but, instead of travelling through outer space, they sail through 'inner space'.

One such deep-sea exploration vehicle is the crewed submersible *Alvin*. Launched in 1964, *Alvin* was the first submersible that could easily roam the deep sea with a human crew aboard. *Alvin* carries three people inside a small sphere with solid titanium walls and small portholes. It can descend to 4.5 kilometers (2.8 miles) below the surface.

If you regard the deep sea as inner space, *Alvin* certainly looks like a spacecraft—enhanced by a collection of lights, manipulator arms and sample baskets. *Alvin* is also like a spacecraft because it carries its own air supply and power supply.

Alvin was built by the United States navy and is operated by the Woods Hole Oceanographic Institute. Other crewed submersibles include *Johnson-Sea-Link* (shown here) and ✈ *Clelia* from the United States, the Japanese submersible ✈ *Shinkai 6500,* the French ✈ *Nautile* and the Russian *Mir* submersibles.

Profile of a deep-sea scientist

Dr. Cindy Lee Van Dover

As a child, Cindy Lee Van Dover thought that all the world was known and there was nowhere left to explore. That was before she discovered the deep sea—a frontier for both science and exploration. It is still a place where little is known and much is yet to be discovered. While she was still at school, Cindy Lee Van Dover read about the deep-sea submersible *Alvin* and dreamed of being aboard it. As an adult, she achieved this dream.

Dr. Van Dover discovered a type of deep-sea shrimp that had no eyes but could still 'see'. The shrimps swarmed around deep-sea vents in the Atlantic Ocean. Dr. Van Dover noticed two bright spots on their backs. It turned out that these spots were part of larger organs that contained light-sensitive chemicals, and they were linked to the shrimps' brains. At first, there seemed to be no reason why the shrimps needed light-sensitive organs in the total darkness of the deep sea. Dr. Van Dover thought that the hot vents actually glowed in the dark. Using a digital camera on *Alvin*, she proved her theory right.

Humans have only recently begun to venture into the extreme pressure, darkness and chilling cold of the deep sea. From inside the submersible *Alvin*, scientists have a first-hand view of the deep-sea environment, and they can take photographs and bring back samples as well.

Dr. Cindy Lee Van Dover was the 49th person to qualify as a pilot of a deep-sea submersible, but the first woman to do so.

These shrimps crowded around a deep-sea vent have no eyes. They use light-sensitive organs on their backs to find the dull glow of the hot vents.

Exploring new frontiers
Recent discoveries

The discovery of communities that can survive without light has shown us that our world is far more complex than we once thought. It also shows that there is a lot more of the Earth still to explore and many secrets to reveal. Humans have always explored new frontiers, and they will continue to do so.

For example, scientists have only just begun to explore the deep sea. Submersibles that carry humans can only reach 6 kilometers (3.7 miles) below the surface. There is so much more deep ocean beyond our reach. Who knows what will be possible in 10, 20 or even 30 years' time? How much will we have explored 100 years from now?

1960
Jacques Piccard and Donald Walsh descend to the bottom of the ocean, a depth of 10,911 meters (35,797 feet), in a submersible called the *Trieste*.

1969
Neil Armstrong and Buzz Aldrin are the first humans to land on the Moon in the *Apollo 11* Lunar Module, the *Eagle*.

1986

A cave that had been sealed off from the rest of the world was discovered. This cave is home to a range of animals that live totally without sunlight.

1984

The submersible *Johnson-Sea-Link* found life around oil and gas seeps 600 meters (2,000 feet) below the surface.

1977

Geologists aboard the submersible *Alvin* find life around hydrothermal vents 2,500 meters (8,200 feet) below the ocean's surface.

1996

Lake Vostok is discovered below almost 4,000 meters (13,000 feet) of ice in Antarctica. Scientists have yet to drill into the lake itself to see if it contains life.

Future?

Finding out more

Books like this one only give a brief introduction to a subject as broad
as life without sunlight. Some other useful reference books are:

Cindy Lee Van Dover, *The Octopus's Garden*, Helix Books, 1996
David McNab and James Younger, *The Planets*, BBC Books, 1999
John Waters, *Deep-sea Vents: Living Worlds Without Sun*, Cobblehill Books, 1994
Kate Madin, *Down to a Sunless Sea*, Raintree Steck-Vaughan Publishers, 2000
Lynn Margulis and Dorion Sagan, *What is Life?*, Weidenfeld and Nicolson, 1995
Melissa Stewart, *Life Without Sunlight*, Franklin Watts, 1999
Michael Gross, *Life on the Edge*, Plenum Trade, 1996

You may also find the following web sites useful:

www.reston.com/astro/extreme.html
A section of the Astrobiology Web that focuses on life in extreme environments.
It has lots of links and a search facility.

www.resa.net/nasa/onearth_extreme.htm and www.resa.net/nasa/otherextreme.htm
Two web sites with descriptions of various extremophiles, and a series of links.

www.marine.whoi.edu/ships/ships_vehicles.htm
Web site of the Deep Sea Operations Group at Woods Hole Oceanographic Institute.
Go to the sections on *Alvin*, ROVs and AUVs.

www.bio.psu.edu/cold_seeps/cover.html
A site called Life Without Light. It is a tour through the cold-seep habitats
in the Gulf of Mexico.

www.ucmp.berkeley.edu/alllife/threedomains.html
A very comprehensive site about Life on Earth. Have a look at the section
on the Archaea.

photojournal.jpl.nasa.gov
NASA photographs of planets and moons. Take a little time to explore Mars and Europa.

As urls (web site addresses) may change, you may have trouble finding a site
listed here. If this happens, you can still use the key words highlighted throughout
the book to search for information about a topic.

Glossary

Archaea: A group of bacteria that has recently been discovered. Most are extremophiles. They are also called the Archaebacteria

astrobiologists: Scientists who specialize in looking for life beyond Earth

bacteria: Single-celled microscopic organisms

community: All the organisms found in an area at a particular time

environment: All external conditions and factors, living and non-living, that affect an organism

extreme environment: A place where it is hard for organisms to survive because it is very hot, very cold, or very dry

geologists: Scientists who study the Earth and its rocks

habitat: The place where a group (community) of different organisms lives under a particular set of environmental conditions

hydrogen: An explosive gas

hydrogen sulphide: A gas that is made of hydrogen and sulphur. It smells like rotten eggs. It is poisonous to most life on Earth

hydrothermal vents: Hot springs that are found in volcanic regions of the ocean floor

methane: An explosive gas that is made of hydrogen and carbon

microbiologists: Scientists who specialize in the study of microbes

microscopic: Too small to be seen without a microscope

organic: A substance produced by a living thing

organisms: Living things

photosynthesis: A process that uses sunlight to combine carbon dioxide and water to make sugars (food) and oxygen

seep: To ooze out slowly

Index